Mountains In My Stride

by James Facos

A Baker's Plays Acting Edition

Single copies of plays are sold for reading purposes only. The copying or duplicating of a play, or any part of play, by hand or by any other process, is an infringement of the copyright. Such infringement will be vigorously prosecuted.

Baker's Plays
7611 Sunset Blvd.
Los Angeles, CA 90042
bakersplays.com

NOTICE

This book is offered for sale at the price quoted only on the understanding that, if any additional copies of the whole or any part are necessary for its production, such additional copies will be purchased. The attention of all purchasers is directed to the following: This work is protected under the copyright laws of the United States of America, in the British Empire, including the Dominion of Canada, and all other countries adhering to the Universal Copyright Convention. Violations of the Copyright Law are punishable by fine or imprisonment, or both. The copying or duplication of this work or any part of this work, by hand or by any process, is an infringement of the copyright and will be vigorously prosecuted.

This play may not be produced by amateurs or professionals for public or private performance without first submitting application for performing rights. Royalties are due on all performances whether for charity or gain, or whether admission is charged or not. Since performance of this play without the payment of the royalty fee renders anybody participating liable to severe penalties imposed by the law, anybody acting in this play should be sure, before doing so, that the royalty fee has been paid. Professional rights, reading rights, radio broadcasting, television and all mechanical rights, etc. are strictly reserved. Application for performing rights should be made directly to BAKER'S PLAYS.

No one shall commit or authorize any act or omission by which the copyright of, or the right to copyright, this play may be impaired. No one shall make any changes in this play for the purpose of production.

Publication of this play does not imply availability for performance. Both amateurs and professionals considering a production are strongly advised in their own interest to apply to Baker's Plays for written permission before starting rehearsals, advertising, or booking a theatre.

Whenever the play is produced, the author's name must be carried in all publicity, advertising and programs. Also, the following notice must appear on all printed programs, "Produced by special arrangement with Baker's Plays."

Licensing fees for *MOUNTAINS IN MY STRIDE* is based on a per performance rate and payable one week in advance of the production.

Please consult the Baker's Plays website at www.bakersplays.com or our current print catalogue for up to date licensing fee information.

Copyrights 1969; renewed 1997, as A DAY OF GENESIS
Copyright © 2009 by James Facos
Made in U.S.A.
All rights reserved.

MOUNTAINS IN MY STRIDE
ISBN 978-0-87440-313-8
#1861-B

CHARACTERS

(In the order of their appearance)

McIVER - a wiry, forceful, energetic man of 40 or so.

SARY - a thin-boned, tight-mannered, grasping and cash-hard woman of 39 or so.

HAWKINS - a burly, good-natured, obliging hulk of a man.

BAILEY - a very spirited, young river man.

JORY BULLARD - a burly bull of a man.

JASON HUNT - a tall, rugged, weather-tanned man in his early 30s. His movements are quiet and easy. He wears a shirt of homespun, fringed buckskin britches, and moccasins.

HANNAH WEBSTER - a tall, poised woman of 35 or so, her propriety not yet hardened into primness.

RUTH TOBY - a gentle and lovely woman of 22 or so, on the threshold of self-discovery. Her dress is a heavy black mourning dress.

BLUNDER - a sinewy man, clad in buckskin revealing a compact, muscular body. A knife sheath hangs from his belt. His movements are supple, with cat-like grace, an almost primitive swiftness in them. He seems older than his years only because of his shaggy beard.

TOM BOWIE - a bulky giant of a man, weathered and hard-built, in homespun shirt, leather britches and heavy boots, muddy with travel. In his early, rugged 40s.

A crowd of McIver's men, and river and town folk.

ACT ONE

Scene One

*(**TIME:** A chill March morning, shortly after sunrise – towards the early 1830s.)*

*(**SCENE:** Sary's Place: a frontier general store – low-raftered, rough-planked, and sturdy – on the west bank of the Missouri.)*

(Downstage right, a door leading to the back quarters. A table heaped with pelts – loose and bundled – and piled beneath. Some bales to one side by the door. A stout chair.)

(Back wall: shelves to the rafters, packed tight with bottles, tins, packets, jugs, etc. Left, a window, its heavy wooden weather-hatch down.)

(Stage left, along the wall, crates and bales; then a timbered door leading to the outside road. A low bench by the door.)

(Rear stage to center: a counter before the wall shelves. On it, a worn, well-thumbed ledger and a rusted, inaccurate scale to one side. Barrels and bins, big and little, lined before the counter.)

*(**AT RISE:** The only light comes from a flickering oil lamp on the table [the pelts have been pushed to the floor in a heap]. **McIVER** lies slumped over the table, asleep. A scattering of papers around him.)*

*(The door to the back opens, and **SARY** comes out brusquely and crosses to the window. She raises the hatch and sunlight streams through. **McIVER** wakens and stretches as **SARY** goes briskly about readying for business.)*

SARY. Sorry, McIver. You can't have this room no more.

McIVER. I know, Sary. Business is business.

SARY. You been up all night?

McIVER. *(rising and putting out the oil lamp)* I didn't know it was morning so fast.

SARY. What's yer wife goin' t' say?

McIVER. Probably hallelujia.

SARY. I got t' get t' the Creek fer water, so mind the place, will ye?

(She bustles out, SR, as a hard, impatient knocking shakes the outside door, SL.)

HAWKINS. *(off-stage)* Hey, McIver! Open 'er up!

*(**McIVER** crosses and unbolts the door. The cold, silvery light of morning streams in as **HAWKINS** struggles with a long, unwieldy package wrapped in burlap and tied with a stout cord.)*

McIVER. Anyone see ye?

HAWKINS. Nope. Just like ye said. We did it all secret-like.

(Tugs impatiently at the cord.)

'Course, it ain't perfessional, none. But it do look big.

McIVER And the other ones?

HAWKINS. The boys got 'em cached away. They'll put 'em up t'night soon's you give the word.

(With a sharp jerk, he breaks the cord, pulls the wrappings away, and unfolds a massive banner along the counter: JASON HUNT FOR CONGRESS.)

Miss Ruth – she done the spelling fer us.

McIVER. It sure do look good.

HAWKINS. Where will it go?

McIVER. Right over the band-stand so's everybody can see it.

HAWKINS. That ain't sayin' they'll know what it says.

McIVER. They will when we get done with 'em.

HAWKINS. Reckon Lawyer Craig's got signs like this, too?

McIVER. Don't see why not.

(He starts to set the pelt table in order again, moving the oil lamp to the counter and piling the pelts on the table.)

HAWKINS. Not big as this 'un, I bet. Reckon Jason'll like it?

McIVER. Well, that's the question now, ain't it?

HAWKINS. What if'n he don't want t' run?

McIVER. He will if we have t' hog-tie him and drag him to Congress ourselves!

HAWKINS. I don't know. You can lead a hoss t' water, but –

McIVER. If we make it deep enough – and throw him in – he'll have t' swim fer it.

HAWKINS. It'd be easier if'n we'd get him elected first, an' then kinda told him about it.

McIVER. Well, maybe that'll be just the way.

(As BAILEY appears in the doorway, stage left.)

Yeah, Bailey?

BAILEY. Me and the boys're waiting on ye.

McIVER. Ye got the lumber?

BAILEY. Yeah. Across the way.

McIVER. Then start the stand going.

BAILEY. We got the fiddlers fer the dancin' later. And Shorty's got his squeeze-box. And Abe Tyler – he's got his ol' bugle –

McIVER. How many men ye got out there now?

BAILEY. Well, six fer the stand. The rest're just settin' 'round.

McIVER. *(Crosses to the table and picks up a sheet of paper from the pelts.)* I want Jeb Hollister, Kanin, and Styver t' ride out t' these folks – and remind 'em about the meetin' t'night.

(He hands BAILEY the sheet.)

Tell the others t' wait on me.

(BAILEY takes the list and, with a nod, turns and goes.)

McIVER. *(Turning to HAWKINS.)* Now, there's only the flags and things.

HAWKINS. I'll get 'em fer ye.

McIVER. They're 'cross the way at Granny Rogers's place. I got t' go t' Parson's Ridge and pick up the family.

HAWKINS. Ye know, McIver, with the way you work things out, I got a feelin' – if ye'd a-set yer mind to it real hard-like – you could-a gotten Benedict Arnold hisself fer president.

McIVER. Maybe – if'n I believed in him the way –

(*Suddenly, offstage left, shouts: "Fight!" – "Hey, watch it!" – "Look at 'em go!"*)

(**HAWKINS** *bolts for the door.*)

HAWKINS. It's Jason! – And Jory Bullard – !

(**McIVER** *leaps to the door.*)

HAWKINS. Look out, Jason! He's grabbin' fer the chain – !

McIVER. Jason! Don't – !

HAWKINS. (*Leaping back.*) Watch it, McIver! Here they come – !

(**McIVER** *leaps back as* **JORY BULLARD** *whirls crashing back into the room. He slams against a crate and slumps to the floor. He tries to rise, but sinks again, beaten – his clothes torn, his face bleeding.*)

(*Slowly* **JASON HUNT** *sags to the doorway, panting and bloody-faced. He leans against the door-frame, looking down at* **JORY**.)

McIVER. Jason – ?

JASON. (*Crosses to* **JORY**. *He kneels down and grabs* **JORY** *roughly by the shirt front.*) Now, Jory – you go back and tell that belly-crawling Craig if'n I ever hear o' you threatening anybody again – ever! – I'll squash you both so flat, you'll have t' take off yer boots t' see daylight.

(*He drags* **JORY** *stumbling to his feet and shoves him towards the door.*)

Now, get – !

(*With a push and a well placed boot.*)

– before I lose my temper!

(*To* **McIVER**, *still keyed up, as* **JORY** *sails out.*)

I don't mind Craig's buying votes, ye understand. Some o' the folks here could use the money. But – But, Jory – tellin' folks that if'n they didn't vote fer Craig, they'd be findin' their fields burnt – or their hogs killed. Things like that – !

McIVER. *(Guiding* **JASON** *to the chair.)* Ye'd better sit over here so's we can fix you up.

HAWKINS. We sure don't want folks thinkin' we had t' beat ye up t' run.

*(***JASON** *cuts him a quick look.)*

*(***McIVER** *goes behind the counter, searching the shelves, and finds a bottle of liniment. He takes out his bandana and, uncorking the bottle, spills liniment onto the cloth, going to* **JASON**.*)*

McIVER. One thing: he didn't do as much as them renegades did t' ye last spring.

HAWKINS. That where ye was tomahawked, Jason?

McIVER. How about gettin' them flags from Granny Rogers?

HAWKINS. Sure, McIver. Right away.

(He hurries out, stage left.)

McIVER. *(Looking over* **JASON**'s *cuts.)* Next time, Jason, you leave me and the boys take care o' things like Jory. You could've gotten yerself messed up that way.

JASON. 'Pears like you and the boys've been taking care of a lot of things.

McIVER. Could be. Can't help what folks want. And that's that.

JASON. Even if I don't?

McIVER. Don't ye, Jason?

(A beat.)

JASON. I don't know, McIver. I really don't know.

McIVER. *(Starts daubing at and cleaning up the cuts, his voice slow and true.)* Jason, listen to me now – Yer father – Judge Hunt – was the finest man I ever knowed. I never knew there'd be two of the same kind.

(JASON reacts to the sting of the liniment.)

You just keep quiet fer a spell. I seen you growing up – just like any other boy around here. Hunting in the woods. Kicking up your heels around town. I didn't think much o' ye then. No more'n most people did... And then – that time I saw you in the woods – alone, reading – Remember? I never forgot that. It was like I'd caught me a sight o' something – like once when I seen a deer being borned, and I was the only one t' see it.

(He turns back to the counter for more liniment, thoughtful with memory as he talks.)

And when ye went to Virginia t' school, I thought on that day in the woods. I don't know why. It just stuck with me. And that summer yer Pa died and you came back, I thought you'd be takin' *his* place. But ye didn't –

(He comes back to JASON and again cleans and daubs the cuts.)

You went west, so I figgered, well, that was the end of it...until the last time you come back, and we started t' talk on things.

(Finished with the cuts, McIVER wipes his hands and goes back to the counter, to put the liniment away.)

I'd been a farmer, Jason. All my life I've been a farmer. Living day by day, fighting the earth, seeing no more than my own fields. And then you started a-talking about the country you'd seen...It's a young country, you said, and a-growing. And its roots be young. And they have to be cared for and set straight and nourished – to be strong and deep – fer the tree to grow t' bear good fruit...I understood yer, language, Jason. And I understood more 'cause, suddenly – fer the first time in my life – I started t' think on all the fields this country could be – of all the land and the people in it. And *I* wanted t' do all I could t' keep them roots straight and strong like you said.

(Coming back to face **JASON** *squarely.)*

And the best way, Jason, is to have men like you where the roots really are – in the government. What you've done for me, Jason – in your words, in the way you think – you can do for others. What you've given me, you can give them – !

*(***JASON*** *starts up, tensed, on the taut brink of struggle.)*

McIVER. *(Sharply.)* Or do ye want fer Craig to be there – eatin' his way through them roots, t' fatten hisself?

JASON. No. But I got me a dream, McIver.

McIVER. Bigger than Congress?

JASON. Maybe. For me.

McIVER. And Ruth?

(A beat.)

JASON. I don't know. Ever since her Pa died, she doesn't seem the same any more. Like she was scared o' something –

*(***HAWKINS*** *barges in with a basket filled with bunting, streamers of red, white, and blue piled high.)*

HAWKINS. Got the flags, McIver.

(He drops the basket and fumbles around for a folded flag. He holds it out to **McIVER.***)*

Granny got this'un out'n her trunk. Says you can use it. It's kinda old, though.

(With **McIVER***'s help, he unfolds it – to find a blazing Tory version of the Union Jack. He catches* **McIVER***'s look.)*

No – huh?

McIVER. Not unless we're running the king of England for Congress.

JASON. Now, that's an idea.

McIVER. A – what?

JASON. Just don't you go foldin' that flag away, McIver. You might be needin' it.

(He goes out, grinning.)

(**McIVER** *looks to* **HAWKINS**; *then, with an abrupt nod, drops his corner of the flag and strides to the door. He calls out across the way.*)

McIVER. Bailey! Tell the boys t' get those signs up. We're starting the campaign now!

(*to* **HAWKINS**)

It's time to get that water high.

(*CURTAIN*)

Scene Two

(*TIME: An hour later.*)

(**SARY** *is behind the counter, weighing bacon for* **HANNAH**. **RUTH** *stands by the open doorway, staring off, preoccupied, a half-haunted look in her eyes. A small pile of books is on the bench by the door. Quickly* **SARY** *snatches the bacon from the scales and, wrapping it deftly, slides it to the rest of the parcels on the counter and smiles up at* **HANNAH**.)

SARY. Bacon.

HANNAH. (*Checks it off a list.*) Bacon. I guess that does it, Sary.

SARY. Need any flour?

HANNAH. (*Turning to* **RUTH**.)

Ruth?...Ruth?

(**RUTH** *looks to her.*)

Need any flour?

RUTH. I don't think so.

SARY. If ye do, ye'd better get it now. I'm near out of it.

(*Packing the parcels into a small box.*)

Fact is, I'm near out of everything these days.

RUTH. It's a long way west, Sary.

SARY. A long way between stores, I tell 'em. Makes 'em want t'buy more that way.

HANNAH. (*Counting out money from her purse.*) Even at these prices?

SARY. A body's got t' look t' the future, don't they?

HANNAH. Not everybody, Sary.

SARY. (*Putting the money into a heavy cash-box from under the counter. About the parcels:*) You gonna go back with these now?

HANNAH. No. I'll wait with Ruth. There's not much time now.

RUTH. Why not come to the school with me, Hannah? You could take some of the children – just for the morning –

HANNAH. Me?! No. No, thank you.

RUTH. You'd make a fine teacher, Hannah.

HANNAH. I'll think of it...back in Boston.

SARY. Ye know, Hannah. That's almost funny – you going east. Everybody else seems t' be goin' west.

HANNAH. That, Sary, is' the story of my life.

RUTH. The Rankins are leaving next week.

SARY. West? But they're settled here. They been here five years. Why're they goin'?

RUTH. I don't know, Sary. There's something in the wind – a light in the sky –

SARY. Hogwash!

RUTH. You should've seen Tony yesterday. Little Tony Rankin. He came up right after lessons to tell me he wouldn't be around next week to ring the schoolbell. "We're going west, Miss Toby," he said. And the look in his eyes – filled with sparks of wildfire. And the way he swaggered away – as if he were ten feet tall and twenty-seven instead of – such a small boy who just learned to spell his name.

SARY. Well, one thing's fer sure. For everyone that's a-goin', they's more a-comin'. We're gonna be a big city one o' these days. Look at yer Jason there. Gonna get t' Congress –

RUTH. If he'll run.

SARY. Oh, he'll run, right enough. Besides, everybody's for him, ain't they? All Lawyer Craig's got's his slippery words and them politician friends o' his'n. But Jason there – he's done things – like goin' all the way t' Californy and comin' back – three times already. He's got the know-how, Jason has. He knows what folks need – And Congress is gonna know, too, when he gets there. Just wait 'til that big meetin' t'night. You'll see.

(to **HANNAH***)*

Too bad you ain't gonna be there, Hannah.

HANNAH. I know. But I've already made my plans. The boat's due in this noon, and I'm taking it back.

SARY. You couldn't wait on the next one, huh?

HANNAH. No. I never change my plans.

SARY. I'll get Blunder t' tote these out fer ye.

(She crosses to the window.)

Hey, Blunder!

(to HANNAH)

Boston's a far piece out, ain't it?

HANNAH. Yes, Sary. Quite a far piece.

SARY. Further than Californy?

HANNAH. No. Not so far.

SARY. But it's still a long ride, ain't it? I mean, once ye get t' the other side the river.

HANNAH. Yes, Sary. A long, long ride.

SARY. BLUNDER! You wait here. I'll get 'im. Ever since he come back from Jefferson, he don't seem the same no more.

(She storms out, stage left.)

(A beat.)

HANNAH. It's all right for me to go now, isn't it? You'll be all right?

RUTH. I'll be all right. And, Hannah, thanks for coming out here – to be with me.

HANNAH. He was my favorite uncle. I was glad to see him before – the end.

RUTH. I couldn't have gone through it without you, Hannah…and staying all these months.

HANNAH. What's three months to a Bostonian like me? When I get back, it'll all be the same. Like dropping a stitch in knitting. The pattern's there. All I do is pick it up…just where I left off.

RUTH. It sounds so warm when you say that. So solid and safe –

HANNAH. Ruth…come back with me.

RUTH. Sometimes I want to go back to Boston. I think of being young there – the way it was – with Mama and all my friends – Hannah – sometimes it's so – so piercing, I can't even cry to get rid of it! I think of the things we did...with every day safe and in its place. And knowing for certain, that after Sunday, Monday would come, with Monday things to do.

HANNAH. Some people need patterns, Ruth.

RUTH. But then – when Papa came out here – after Mama died – I felt excited – going new places – doing new things. Even now – every time I hear a wagon rolling through, the cracking of the whips, the shouting – knowing they're going west – knowing they're a part of something big and growing, I want to go, too. I want to shout: Wait for me! Let me go, too! – But I don't. I only sit and fold my hands, and listen...and something inside me turns to stone...and I can't even move.

HANNAH. Have you told Jason all this?

RUTH. No.

HANNAH. He cares, doesn't he?

RUTH. I don't know.

HANNAH. Maybe getting tomahawked last spring didn't help him any.

RUTH. He'd have gone west again if that hadn't happened. Him and Tom.

HANNAH. I know. Jason told me. And the strange, far places they had found together –

RUTH. Wilderness places no man had ever seen before.

(Turning. Tensed.)

Hannah, have you ever heard the cry of an eagle?

*(Suddenly, stage left, **BLUNDER** spins stumbling through the doorway, sparking injured fire. **SARY** stomps in behind, brandishing a long, glittering hunting knife.)*

BLUNDER. Stop pushin'. It's agin a man's dingity –

SARY. You ain't got no "dingity" –

(With a snort, she stabs the knife heavily into the counter.)

– whittling all day –

BLUNDER. Hey, that's my knife – !

*(He goes for it, but **SARY** steps in between him and it.)*

SARY. *(Gesturing to the parcels.)* After ye get these taken keer of.

BLUNDER. Honestly, Sary – one o' these days I'm gonna give up a-courtin' ye.

SARY. Ha!

BLUNDER. *(To* **HANNAH.***)* She's enough t' drive me back to the Pawnee agin –

HANNAH. The Pawnee – ?

BLUNDER. Mighty fine people, the Pawnee. Growed up with 'em, purty near – back'a-ways. But kinda sensitive, like. Had t' leave 'em, ye know. Special in-vite-tation o' the chief –

SARY. Blunder! One more o' yer blasted lies –

BLUNDER. 'Tain't no lie! Got into trouble with his daughter, 'pears like.

HANNAH. Blunder!

BLUNDER. Well, it's the truth, ain't it?

SARY. You wouldn't know the truth if it stared ye in the face till ye was cross-eyed.

BLUNDER. No?!

SARY. *(To* **HANNAH.***)* Did ye hear 'im tell about Broken Moon yet?

HANNAH. Broken Moon?

RUTH. *(Caught.)* On the war-path again?!

BLUNDER. Not this side the Happy-Huntin'-Grounds he ain't.

SARY. 'Course not, Ruthie. Blunder here – he's done kilt 'im, he says.

RUTH. Is that the truth, Blunder? Is Broken Moon dead?

BLUNDER. Him an' five others.

RUTH. When?

BLUNDER. The other day. On my way back from Jefferson.

RUTH. But why didn't *you* tell us?

BLUNDER. I told Sary there. I figgered if'n she knowed, then everybody'd know.

SARY. I wouldn't tell a lie like that to a dead hound!

RUTH. Is it a lie, Blunder?

SARY. Sure, Blunder. Tell 'er what you told me. Tell 'er how ye did it.

BLUNDER. With my ol' fiddle.

(As **RUTH** *turns away, hurt.)*

Honest! So help me Hannah!

HANNAH. I refuse!

BLUNDER. They shot their arrys at me, so's all I did was — shoot 'em back.

SARY. With yer fiddle.

BLUNDER. The fiddle strings. I just stretched them arrys acrost my fiddle strings and — *wham*! 'Course, I busted a few strings —

HANNAH. Blunder —

BLUNDER. *(Fiercely.)* I got proof!

SARY. What proof?

(BLUNDER *looks at her, hesitates — then, lowering his head, takes up the parcels — and knife — and starts out, silent. At the door, stage left, he turns, his voice rusty.)*

BLUNDER. I got proof.

(He turns and goes out, sulking.)

RUTH. If only it had been true —

SARY. It ain't safe fer anyone out there. Can't all be lucky like Jason. 'Course, he was massacreed up a bit in the fightin'. But he got through. Not like them others they'd found.

HANNAH. *(Wonderingly.)* Blunder got through.

SARY. Only 'cause injuns think idiots're something special. Won't touch hide ner hair of 'em.

RUTH. I wonder if Tom —

SARY. *(Behind the counter, sorting pelts.)* The day Tom Bowie don't get though, be the day I'll be president.

RUTH. But he should have been here yesterday.

SARY. Don't know why he's comin', eh? —

RUTH. No. Blunder just said he wanted to see Jason.

HANNAH. To go west again?

(**RUTH** *reacts sharply.*)

SARY. *(Curiously, to* **HANNAH.***)* You interested? In Tom, I mean?

HANNAH. Sary, how could I be – "interested"? I've never met the man.

SARY. But ye heared of him, right? And it's natural, ain't it? He's a man. You're a woman.

HANNAH. I'm also from Boston.

SARY. Women need men in Boston, too, don't they?

HANNAH. *Some* do.

SARY. And you don't?

HANNAH. Let's just say, Sary, that I've never met the kind of man I needed.

SARY. Hogwash! A man's a man –

RUTH. What kind of man would he have been, Hannah?

HANNAH. Would have been?

(A beat.)

Oh, when I was seventeen, I thought I'd marry a man who – a man who could take mountains in his stride. Only – there aren't any mountains in Boston.

SARY. Then why go back?

HANNAH. Patterns, Sary. They help – when you're not seventeen any more.

SARY. *(Taking the pelts to the table.)* Ye're all packed, then?

HANNAH. Yes, Sary. I'm all packed.

SARY. Then I don't reckon ye'd be needin' anything?

HANNAH. I don't know. A small trunk – a traveling chest? Mine's an old one. The cover's cracked and – I was wondering if it'd hold for the trip back.

SARY. Well, I'm pure outta trunks, Hannah – 'ceptin' a few I brung out here myself when I come –

HANNAH. No –

SARY. I won't be needin' 'em none. And they's sure strong. Like t'see 'em? They're right in back –

HANNAH. I don't –

SARY. Let ye have 'em fer next t' nothing – almost.

(She is about to lead HANNAH out back when JASON enters, SL.)

Well, if'n it ain't the next congressman hisself! Howdy, Jason.

(JASON, brushed up now, flicks SARY a cheery wave, glancing from her to HANNAH and RUTH – who looks at him tautly.)

JASON. Howdy, Sary. Hannah. Ruth.

SARY. You look kinda banged up a bit, Jason.

JASON. It sure didn't pretty me up none, did it?

SARY. From what I hear, Jory ain't exactly the picture o' health, neither. Do it hurt?

JASON. No more'n it feels.

(to RUTH)

Ruth?

SARY. *(leading HANNAH out, SR)* They's right fine trunks, Hannah. Let me show 'em to you They're just out'n the back shed.

(As HANNAH exits, SARY turns in, the doorway.)

Jason?

JASON. Yeah?

SARY. Ye know that land o' yers. I was figuring – if'n ye went t' Congress, ye wouldn't be needin' it no more, would ye?

JASON. Well, Sary, that's one bridge I aim t' cross when I get to it.

(SARY hesitates, then quickly goes.)

JASON. Blunder said ye'd be here.

RUTH. *(Coldly.)* I didn't see you last night.

JASON. I was on Glory Peak.

RUTH. All night?

JASON. Thinking.

RUTH. And?

JASON. I saw McIver this morning. 'Pears you two've been doing some mighty fancy planning, don't it?

(A beat.)

Ruth, why are you so all-fired set on me goin' t' Congress?

RUTH. Because I believe in you – like everybody else around here. And you yourself said you wanted to help them –

JASON. Sure! But I never said anything about Congress –

RUTH. What better place than Congress? It's your duty, Jason. Your calling –

JASON. Is it, Ruth? Or is it something else?

RUTH. Something else?

JASON. Ruth…remember last week? The way we stood – just the two of us – high on Glory Peak, with nothing before us but sky and hills. You stared with the strangest light in your eyes – as if you'd never seen the world so wide before. And then – suddenly – high above us – the wild screaming of the eagle – like something fierce and alive, crying out in ourselves. And we looked up and saw that eagle circling over us and beyond – and then – soaring out across the hills and valleys – and then – after all that time – we looked at each other –

RUTH. And came down.

JASON. But *changed*, Ruth –

RUTH. No, Jason. I am exactly the same!

JASON. Are you, Ruth?

RUTH. It – was just the surprise of it all. I'd – I'd never heard an eagle cry before –

JASON. But you did hear it, then –

*(A beat, as **RUTH** turns away from him rigidly.)*

You know – I had me a feeling, Ruth, that on Glory Peak something happened. To both of us, I thought. Something like us both knowing the same dream. A real, exciting dream come suddenly true – or could be.

(A beat, as **RUTH** *stands unmoved.)*

And then we came down again!

RUTH. *(Turning. Fearful.)* Jason – do you love me?

JASON. *(Angrily.)* Yes! I do!

*(***BLUNDER*** barges in, stage left, bellowing.)*

BLUNDER. Jason! Looky who's here!

*(***JASON*** and* **RUTH** *turn as* **TOM BOWIE** *stands grinning in the doorway, with full pack and long rifle in hand.)*

JASON. Tom! Tom Bowie!

TOM. Howdy, Jason. Hi-ya, Ruthie.

RUTH. *(Crossing to him.)* Tom – it's wonderful –

TOM. Enough fer a kiss?

RUTH. Enough for two.

(Kissing him on both cheeks.)

TOM. Now, that's what I call being right generous.

BLUNDER. Wished I had that way with wimmen.

JASON. *(Helping* **TOM** *unsling his pack.)* Here – let's get rid o' this.

TOM. *(To* **BLUNDER.***)* Ain't you done hitched Sary yet?

BLUNDER. Nope.

TOM. All ye need's a whole passel o' money and stuff –

BLUNDER. *(Setting himself down on a keg, toying with his knife.)* Been so busy a-courtin' 'er, I ain't had no time t' make me no money.

TOM. Maybe she ain't the right woman fer ye, then.

BLUNDER. O, she's the right woman – Leastways, I reckon she's the right 'un. Ain't she?

TOM. Danged if I know, Blunder.

BLUNDER. But how can ye know? You ever found the right one, Tom?

TOM. Nope.

BLUNDER. Then how ye gonna tell if'n ye do?

TOM. *(Stretching, easing the ache of his muscles.)* O, I kind a figure she'll have a sort of a – a light in her eyes.

BLUNDER. A light?

TOM. Like noonday stars.

BLUNDER. But – they ain't no such thing as noonday stars.

TOM. *(With a laugh.)* There will be, Blunder.

BLUNDER. Sary's got a squint in hers.

(As, stage right, **SARY** *enters, suddenly seeing* **TOM.***)*

SARY. Of all the no 'count, windy-footed varmints! Tom Bowie!

(She rushes to him. He swings her up and around and sets her down again.)

TOM. Hi-ya, Sary-gal.

SARY. Gosh and a-goshen – you sure do be lookin' prime, Tom.

*(***TOM*** is suddenly caught by the sight of* **HANNAH** *coming in. There is an almost visible spark of shock as their eyes meet)*

RUTH. Tom... my cousin. Hannah Webster. From Boston.

TOM. *Miss* Webster.

HANNAH. *(Extending her hand.)* Mr. Bowie.

TOM. *(With a slight bow, still holding her look.)* It pleasures me, m'am.

HANNAH. The pleasure, Mr. Bowie – is all mine.

SARY. Thought ye'd be in yesterday, Tom. Tom?

TOM. They was things t' get ready back in Jefferson... held me up.

(Self-consciously **HANNAH** *turns away from his look as* **SARY** *slips behind the counter and comes up with a jug and a tin cup. She uncorks the jug and starts to pour.)*

SARY. Thought it'd be Broken Moon.

TOM. Broken Moon?! Ain't ye heared? He's long gone, Sary.

SARY. *(Slops a spill.)* Dead?!

TOM. Him and five others. Just outside Jefferson.

HANNAH. *(A look to* **BLUNDER,** *his knife now sheathed as he picks at a bale.)* When?

TOM. Hard t' say. A few days ago maybe.

SARY. How?

TOM. *(After a swig.)* Knifed. All of 'em. Knifed in the back.

SARY. *(To* **BLUNDER.***)* And you with yer fiddle, eh?

TOM. Fiddle?

SARY. Says he kilt Broken Moon.

TOM. Blunder?

SARY. With a fiddle, he says –

TOM. A – what?

BLUNDER. *(Glaring to* **SARY.***)* Well, it sounded good, didn't it?

TOM. Almost as good as what the injuns say.

SARY. The injuns?

TOM. They think it's a spirit done it. The one they call Thunder Knife.

JASON. Thunder Knife?!

TOM. Just a legend o' theirs. I heared about it back in Pawnee country.

BLUNDER. Quite a far piece up that-away, ain't it? 'Minds o' the time –

JASON. How come you knew they'd been killed, Blunder?

BLUNDER. *(A beat.)* I – I done found 'em in the woods on my way back.

SARY. Ha! Might-a knowed it!

(To **TOM.***)*

Where ye bunkin' t'night, Tom?

TOM. I ain't, Sary.

SARY. You ain't?!

JASON. You're not staying, Tom?

TOM. No, Jason. Ye see, I – I had t' find out something first. I heared about ye running fer Congress.

JASON. I – was thinking on it.

TOM. Serious-like?

RUTH. Why, Tom?

TOM. Well, up in Jefferson, Jason – there's a lot o' folks aimin' on going west. They's four wagon trains already, just a-settin' and a-waitin' on someone t' lead them, Jason. An' we're the only ones in this whole territory knows the way. They've got a chance with us if'n we lead 'em. I'm takin' two anyway. That's why I've got t' get back afore mornin'. They're joining together. But – the others – They wanted t' know if I could get you t' take 'em through. We'd all go together. All four trains in one big –

RUTH. *(Seeing JASON's face.)* Jason!

TOM. I know it's askin' a lot, Jason. I mean – if'n it's Congress ye want – if'n ye're sure –

RUTH. Tom – tonight there's going to be a meeting. Jason's got to – Tom, he can help these people here more. He can't –

JASON. *(Sharply.)* Ruth!

(**RUTH** *stands staring at him, then slowly freezes in a cold, still blaze as, off-stage, the ringing of the schoolbell fills the silence.*)

RUTH. *(Turning, goes to the bench and picks up her books.)* I'm sorry, Tom. The school –

(She goes towards the door, stage left.)

JASON. Ruth?

(For a moment she stands in the doorway, rigid, unable to move; then forces herself to walk out as the schoolbell rings slowly.)

(CURTAIN)

Scene Three

(*TIME: Mid-afternoon.*)

(*Offstage, noises of steady hammering. Some shouting, indistinct. An occasional fiddle twanging, scraping fragments of jig music.*)

(**JASON** *stands by the window, staring out, lost deep in thought, as* **BLUNDER**, *broom in hand, awkwardly sweeps the floor, mumbling half to* **JASON**, *more to himself.*)

BLUNDER. – says I act like an injun. How'm I supposed t' act? Wasn't till I was ten I knowed I wasn't an injun. Never could figger white folks ways. Makes me feel pure foolish. Maybe I should-a stayed an injun. Leastways I knowed how t' act with 'em –

(*Stage right, the door opens and* **TOM** *comes in, sleepy eyed and stretching, his hair tousled, his shirt open. He stands a moment, working the sleep from his shoulders.*)

BLUNDER. 'Bout time ye woke up. Sleep good?

TOM. Yep. Considerin' that dang-fool rumpus out there. Howdy, Jason.

(*Crosses to the doorway.*)

JASON. (*A nod.*) Tom.

BLUNDER. They're puttin' up a stand fer t'night's speechifyin'. Sure gonna be some shindig. Flag's a-flyin'. Signs up. Even gonna be dancin' after.

TOM. (*Turning.*) What time is it?

BLUNDER. (*Looks out and around at the sun and shadows.*) 'Bout three now.

TOM. Where's Sary?

BLUNDER. Down t' the landing. She's got stuff comin' in on the boat – if'n it ever gets here.

(*Suddenly, looking out, stage left.*)

Hey, Bailey! wait! I'll help ye –

(*He tosses the broom aside and bolts out.*)

(**TOM** *goes behind the counter and, taking out the jug and a cup, starts to pour himself a drink.*)

TOM. Where ye been all day?

JASON. Out. Talking with people. Listening. Congress talk, mostly. Tom, they're serious on me running. They've got signs all over the place – all up and down the river. They want me t' speak tonight. I told them I would. They – They really want me, Tom. Like they were depending on me.

TOM. They ain't the only ones, Jason.

(A beat.)

JASON. How many folks in that wagon train?

TOM. Altogether? Or just the ones I'm taking?

JASON. How many'll be left if'n I don't go?

TOM. O, 'bout a hundred, I reckon. Hard t' tell, countin' the young 'uns.

JASON. How long they been at Jefferson?

TOM. More'n four months now.

JASON. Just a-waitin'?

TOM. They couldn't start out in the winter.

JASON. If I don't go – reckon they'll try it alone?

TOM. They're right set on reaching that Zion o' theirs. You know as good as me, Jason.

JASON. Yeah. I reckon they will.

*(**TOM** pulls up a chair by the pelt table and settles back, drink in hand.)*

TOM. I didn't promise 'em nothing. I didn't say ye'd be taking 'm. I just said I'd ask ye. So they said – if'n they was a chance –

(A beat.)

If'n it was just showin' 'em the way, Jason, I'd take them myself – all of them. But they's a heap o' misery between here and Zion – more'n one man can rightly handle. Most of them folks're just off'n a farm or out'n a city. Half the men can't shoot straight – Some of the women can, though. – But, Jason – they's the other things –

JASON. I know, Tom. I know – only – if'n it was just me, I'd know what to do.

(A tensing beat.)

The other day Ruth and me, we were up on Glory Peak. And suddenly – high above us – we heard an eagle cryin' – so clear and proud. I felt like that cry came from way down deep inside o' me. I felt like it was me out there, soaring – going west. And I felt I knowed fer sure – as clear and as bright as that cry, I knowed fer sure what I was meant to do.

TOM. To go west.

JASON. To follow that cry. And yet – if I do go – I go alone. And, Tom –

TOM. And if you stay?

JASON. There's Congress. I stand a good chance, Tom. I know that now. The folks're behind me. It isn't just Ruth and McIver anymore. It's people like Uncle Cal and Ol' Man Harris and Granny Rogers. I'd be honored to go, Tom. A man could do big things in Congress – good things to help these people. Craig'd only use them, Tom. Use 'em t' slick his own wheels! – Tom, what would you do?

TOM. I don't know, Jason. All's I know is – if'n ye go by other folks' stars, ye're bound t' get lost.

JASON. She'd be with me, Tom.

TOM. And that cry o' the eagle – ?

*(The held look is broken by **BLUNDER** entering, stage left.)*

BLUNDER. Hey, Jason. Fletcher wants t' see ye outside.

TOM. Fletcher?

JASON. Another o' Craig's side-kicks.

BLUNDER. *(Taking up the broom again.)* About t'night, he says. Won't be just a minute, he says.

*(**JASON** exits, stage left, **TOM** looking after him, wondering.)*

BLUNDER. I never seed the likes o' this before. Folks've been comin' t' town all day, from all over.

(He pauses by the door, motioning.)

See? Looky there, now.

*(As **TOM** rises and crosses.)*

The whole dang McIver tribe from way over Parson's Ridge. One more young'un in that wagon, an' it'd bust wide open.

TOM. Is that Fletcher there with Jason?

BLUNDER. Yep. That's him.

TOM. *(Turning back.)* He's new, ain't he?

BLUNDER. The town's full o' new 'uns. Before ye know it, this here's gonna be the biggest city this side the Missouri.

TOM. That Miss Hannah now – How long she been here?

BLUNDER. Three months. But just visitin', like.

TOM. She got anybody back east?

BLUNDER. All her kinfolk, I reckon. 'Ceptin Ruthie, o' course.

(He sets the broom aside and, finding a loose stick from one of the crates, settles back on a bale and takes out his knife to whittle.)

TOM. *(Sitting at the table again.)* Anybody special, like?

BLUNDER. Special? Never heared o' none. Why?

TOM. Just wondering. Been thinking about 'er. A woman like that, coming all the way here alone. That's quite a long trek, Blunder, fer a lone woman.

BLUNDER. Sary's a lone woman.

*(As **JASON** comes back, stage left.)*

JASON. He wanted t' check on who's going t' speak first t'night. I told him first come, first served.

*(**TOM** hands the tin cup to **JASON** for a refill.)*

BLUNDER. Reckon I got a chance with Sary, Tom?

TOM. She's just money-headed – that's all, Blunder.

BLUNDER. I ain't never had no use for money before.

TOM. *(Caught by* **BLUNDER***'s whittling.)* Like up in Pawnee country? Heard ye used t' live with them Pawnee once.

*(***JASON*** gives* **TOM** *the cup again, then moves off to the window again, lost in thought.)*

BLUNDER. Mebbe.

TOM. I holed up with 'em this winter. 'round the Manitou country. Know it?

BLUNDER. I heared about it.

TOM. Ever knowed a chief called Wild Hawk?

BLUNDER. *(Seeing the floor covered with chips, puts his knife away and again reaches for the broom to sweep up.)* Knowed a lot o' chiefs. Knowed a lot o' hawks, too.

TOM. This one had a daughter. Laughing Sky. The purtiest squaw in the whole dang tribe. Small and dark, with the twinklingest eyes I ever did see.

BLUNDER. *(Sweeping.)* What about 'er?

*(***JASON*** turns, aware of the situation.)*

TOM. Nothing. Had a son, though.

BLUNDER. A son?

TOM. Silver Fox. Claimed his pappy was Thunder Knife.

BLUNDER. Heared they done kilt that Thunder Knife years ago.

TOM. Nope. But they sure aim to if'n they ever catch 'im again.

(To **JASON.***)*

'Peared last time he had all them injuns pure mystified. Had 'em all believing he was The Claw O' the Manitou. Reckon he was, too. 'Peared that man could knife a flea square between the eyes at twenty paces by moonlight. The way Broken Moon was, like –

(As **SARY** *bustles in stage left, brusquely taking off her shawl, snorting.)*

SARY. Blunder telling you that old fool story again?

BLUNDER. I ain't said a word!

SARY. *(Going behind the counter. To* **BLUNDER.***)* There's a keg o' nails out back. They need 'em yonder.

BLUNDER. *(Setting the broom aside.)* Where out back?

SARY. By the shed. Under them crates out there.

*(**BLUNDER** goes out, scowling, stage right.)*

SARY. I swear! That man –

JASON. What about Broken Moon, Tom?

TOM. Nothing. 'Cepting it was pure uncommon the way they found them renegades. All six of 'em. One right after the other, right down the trail from Jefferson. About a hundred paces between. Like they'd been stalked down – picked off – one by one –

SARY. Scalped?

TOM. Nope. The only thing missing – near's anyone could tell – was Broken Moon's neckpiece.

JASON. His neckpiece?

SARY. Now, who'd want a thing like that?

TOM. Another injun maybe. Or a white man that knowed injun ways. There's a powerful big medicine in that there neckpiece, I hear –

BAILEY. *(Offstage, stage left)* Hey, Sary! How about them nails?

SARY. Hold yer britches up! They're a-coming.

(Crossing to open door, stage right.)

Hey, Blunder! Hurry up with them nails!

BLUNDER. *(Offstage. A bellow.)* These crates is heavy!

JASON. Hey, Blunder. I'll give ye a hand.

*(He brushes by **SARY** and goes out, stage right.)*

TOM. Sary, when you two gonna get hitched?

SARY. Who? *Blunder*?!

TOM. Well, the way you been yellin' at him, ye'd think you was hitched already.

SARY. Now, you listen t' me, Tom Bowie, and you listen straight. There ain't never been nothing between Blunder and me –

TOM. Never?

SARY. Never!

TOM. You mean you ain't never taken him down by the Creek yet?

SARY. The Creek?

TOM. You know. "Where the grass is so high an' soft an' sweet" – like ye told me once –

*(As **BLUNDER** stands in the doorway. Stage right, the keg of nails held by both hands.)*

BLUNDER. The Creek?

*(**TOM** and **SARY** startle.)*

Have ye, Tom? Have ye ever been down t' the Creek with 'er?

SARY. 'Course he's never – !

BLUNDER. But they's been others?

SARY. And if they has been, what's that to you?

*(As **JASON** enters – and stops, sensing tension.)*

BLUNDER. Then – ye really don't care none.

SARY. Never said I had! Never said I did!

BLUNDER. But – I thought them was just woman ways.

SARY. Ha!

JASON. *(Sharply.)* Sary!

BLUNDER. You stay out'n this, Jason. A man's got pride.

SARY. If'n ye do have, it's all ye've got.

*(**TOM** rises.)*

BLUNDER. Nope. I've got – things.

*(He sees the keg in his hands and sets it down on a near crate as **TOM** goes to him.)*

TOM. Blunder – I'm sorry –

BLUNDER. It's all right, Tom. 'Twarn't you.

*(He turns and, passing **JASON**, goes out, SR.)*

TOM. I never knowed he was that set on ye.

SARY. I never told him t' be, Tom…

*(**TOM** looks at her, disgusted.)*

TOM. I gotta go wash.

(He passes **JASON** *with a glance.)*

I feel like I need it.

(He exits, stage right.)

*(***JASON** *looks through* **SARY**.*)*

SARY. *(Uneasy.)* He ain't got a cent to his name!

JASON. Maybe he don't count money important.

SARY. Then he's a fool!

JASON. Like me, Sary? I don't crave money, either.

SARY. No? You got the best piece o' bottom land in the valley, ain't ye? That's worth a heap o' money.

JASON. Maybe. But I don't aim on selling it any.

SARY. I'd offer ye a right, fine price fer it, Jason.

JASON. It ain't fer sale, Sary.

(He shoulders the keg of nails.)

It come to me free, and I'll give it away free.

SARY. Give? To who?

JASON. To whoever needs it, I reckon.

SARY. I need it, Jason.

JASON. No, Sary. You just want it.

SARY. What's the difference?

BAILEY. *(Offstage. A bellow.)* Hey, Sary! That stand's gotta go up before t'night!

*(***JASON** *turns by the doort, stage left, and almost collides with* **HANNAH**. *He stands aside as* **HANNAH** *enters with* **RUTH**. **RUTH** *has two dresses draped over her arm. She passes* **JASON**, *frozen-eyed.)*

JASON. Hannah. Ruth?

(No response. He exits, stage left.)

SARY. All set and ready t' go, Hannah?

HANNAH. All ready, Sary. I just came over to ask Blunder to take my trunk to the landing.

SARY. Blunder ain't here just now.

HANNAH. O?

SARY. Ain't no rush, though. The boat's a-comin', but it ain't in yet.

(HANNAH turns to see RUTH staring, disturbed, out the door, stage left, after JASON.)

HANNAH. Ruth?...Ruth?

(RUTH turns, with a start; then – aware of the dresses in her hands – holds them out to HANNAH.)

HANNAH. *(Taking the dresses to SARY.)* These are for you, Sary.

SARY. Fer me? – How much?

HANNAH. Sary! They're a gift.

SARY. Well, thank ye, Hannah.

(She takes the dresses, eagerly fingering the material, as TOM comes from out back, washed and combed. He looks rugged and fresh. His eyes meet HANNAH's, and again there is a subtle vibration between them.)

TOM. Miss Hannah.

HANNAH. Mr. Bowie.

TOM. Ruth.

(as RUTH nods coldly)

SARY. *(Shoving the dresses at TOM.)* Looky, Tom. Looky what Hannah just give me. All the way from Boston.

TOM. Looks might purty.

SARY. *(Holding up a blue dress.)* Help me try this 'un on, will ye, Hannah?

RUTH. *(Quickly.)* I'll help you, Sary.

SARY. I always did want this here blue dress.

(She exits, stage right, with RUTH following. The door closes.)

(A beat.)

TOM. Ye'll be glad t' get back t' Boston, I reckon.

HANNAH. I – think so, Mr. Bowie.

TOM. You like it there, I suppose.

HANNAH. Very much!...Usually. It's – It's where I live. Where I've – always – lived.

TOM. I ain't never been east of Ohio.

(*A beat.*)

What's it like in Boston?

HANNAH. Like? Well there aren't any mountains there. I mean – it's hilly…but there aren't – any mountains – there…. It's a sea-coast town. Quite…. Cloudy at times. Cold and…cloudy…. And time – doesn't mean much there….

TOM. Time?

HANNAH. I mean – there, there seems time for everything. But here – there doesn't seem to be enough…time. – I'm afraid I'm not making sense.

TOM. I think I know what you mean. It's like going across them prairies. There ain't nothing around ye but flat, even land, far's ye can see. You keep traveling and traveling, and ye feel like ye're getting nowheres at all. And then, one day – off in the distance – ye see the mountains. And that's the first time ye know where ye're going. You've got something t' move towards.

HANNAH. Yes, Mr. Bowie. That's precisely it.

TOM. And ye like it in Boston?

HANNAH. I – I don't know. Yes! Of course, I do!…But then, I haven't been to California, Mr. Bowie. They tell me you have.

TOM. Four times already. Almost five. Three times with Jason.

HANNAH. What do you mean "almost five"?

TOM. One train didn't make it. We got hit by injuns about seven miles north of a place called Sante Fe. But six of us got back.

HANNAH. Out of – how many?

TOM. Eighty-three that time.

HANNAH. And you're going again?

TOM. With the help o' the good, kind Lord I am.

HANNAH. Do you like danger that much, Mr. Bowie?

TOM. Danger, Miss Hannah? No, but – I don't rightly know's I could explain it. It's something I never told nobody, not even Jason.

(*A beat.*)

Nine years ago I was planting my south field when I saw it. Tall and beautiful and...all white. A twelve-tine buck as white as snow on the mountains – standing there at the edge o' the woods. And then it was gone, like the flash of a shootin' star. And I took after it – just like that! – But I never found it...I spent forty days in the woods that time, just a-huntin' fer t' see it again. But I never did. And yet – when I come out o' them woods, nothing was the same any more. I'd seen places in there like God had just made. Places other folks only dream about but never find fer themselves.

HANNAH. So all these years you've been looking for that white buck – and finding those places –

TOM. Yep. And tellin' folks about 'em, and bringin' 'em to where their dreams got a chance t' take root an' grow. And every time I see their faces, it makes me feel as if I'd swallered sunlight – as if I were pure cloud-tall and could – well –

HANNAH. Take mountains in your stride?

TOM. Yes, Miss Hannah. A whole range a' mountains. Miss Hannah?

HANNAH. Yes, Mr. Bowie?

TOM. The way ye looked at me just then –

HANNAH. I'm sorry.

TOM. Like noonday stars.

HANNAH. Please, Mr. Bowie –

TOM. And yer hair...It's long, ain't it?

HANNAH. Yes...Quite.

TOM. It'd pleasure me t' see it down...Miss Hannah...

HANNAH. I'm afraid...It'd take too long to put it up again, Mr. Bowie. The – The boat's due in – and I – I haven't the time...!

TOM. Hannah –

(*As, stage right, the door bangs open and* **SARY** *stomps in, in an angry fury, the blue dress held out, torn down* *the middle.* **RUTH** *follows.*)

TOM. *Tarnation!*

SARY. Ain't it just my luck!

(*She thrusts the dress out to* **HANNAH.**)

Look at it! I was so all-fired anxious t' get into it, I tore it clean down t' my knees a-pulling it on. And I wanted it so bad, too.

HANNAH. O, Sary. I'm sorry. Can't it be sewn again.

SARY. I can't sew worth a tin penny. You wouldn't be able t' piece it together, would ye?

HANNAH. I'm afraid I haven't the time, Sary. The boat –

TOM. You could miss it.

(*Suddenly, from offstage right,* **BLUNDER** *bellows.*)

BLUNDER. (*Offstage.*) Hey, Jason! – Jason!

SARY. (*Crossing to door, stage right.*) What the blue thunder ye yellin' out there fer?!

BLUNDER. (*Offstage.*) I want t' see Jason.

SARY. Then why don't ye come in! 'stead o' bellowin' out there like a stuck moose. Hannah wants ye t' take her trunk to the landing.

BLUNDER. (*Offstage.*) Reckon I got time fer that.

(*He enters, wearing a coonskin cap and toting a long rifle. A pelt-covered bundle, tied as a pack, is slung over his back, with a powder horn and a leather pouch hanging by his side. His knife is sheathed.*)

(*There is a seasoned strength of the woodsman about him, a naturalness now as he unslings his pack and lays it on a nearby crate. He sets the gun carefully aside by the wall.*)

HANNAH. (*As he enters.*) Blunder, you going somewhere?

BLUNDER. 'Pears that way. I done packed.

SARY. (*Saracastic.*) Never knew ye had so much.

BLUNDER. Where's Jason?

TOM. Out, helpin' Bailey.

BLUNDER. (*Crossing to door, stage left.*) Hey, Jason!

JASON. *(Offstage.)* Be right with ye, Blunder.

BLUNDER. *(Turning.)* Where's yer trunk, Miss Hannah?

HANNAH. At the cabin, Blunder. You'll find it by the door, with a small bag. Be sure you take that, too, please.

TOM. *(To* **HANNAH.***)* Then ye're really going?

HANNAH. Yes, Mr. Bowie. I don't really – Yes. I am.

(**JASON** *enters, stage left.*)

JASON. Ye wanted t' see me, Blunder?

BLUNDER. *(Uneasy, as the others look on. Then straightening.)* I just wanted t' give ye something.

SARY. You?! Give something?!

BLUNDER. *(Taking a beaded belt from his leather pouch.)* I was gonna give it t' ye tonight at the speechin'. But I don't aim t' be around.

(*As* **JASON** *takes it, wordless.*)

It's a medicine-belt. It's fer good luck. Thought you might need it – mebbe. I done made it myself. Learned it from a medicine-man back a-ways.

SARY. Ye might a-knowed it'd be something like that!

BLUNDER. I knowed it ain't much. But I ain't got nothin' else –

JASON. *(With a warm hand clasp.)* Thank ye, Blunder. I'm mighty 'bliged t' ye.

SARY. You don't believe in them things, do ye Jason?

BLUNDER. He don't have to! I do!

JASON. But where ye going?

BLUNDER. I got t' thinkin' on what Tom was sayin'. About that there Zion place. Never been t' Zion. Thought maybe I'd like t' see it – if'n ye don't mind, Tom.

TOM. Mind, Blunder? I'd admire t' have ye along.

BLUNDER. Thank ye, Tom.

(*With a look to* **SARY.**)

There ain't nothin' t' keep me here now.

(*He goes out, stage left, set.*)

RUTH. *(To* **SARY.***)* You letting him go?

SARY. Ain't no concern o' mine what he does! He ain't worth a dead owl's hoot t' me.

JASON. *(fingering the beaded belt)* Not even with land, Sary? Good, rich bottom land?

SARY. Land? You – You mean yers? Ye'd give it to him?

JASON. I won't be needing it now, no matter what I do. But Blunder there – Strikes me he could've used it, maybe.

SARY. And if he could – ?

JASON. I'd give it to him.

(SARY whirls into action. She tosses the torn dress to HANNAH and bolts across the stage, SL.)

SARY. Mind the store, will ye, Tom?

TOM. Where ye going?

(as SARY darts out, primping up her hair, yelling sweetly: "Blunder. Blunder…wait ….!")

(Offstage, SL.)

TOM. *(watching her from the doorway)* Reckon ye give 'er enough rope, Jason?

JASON. Just about.

HANNAH. *(suddenly aware)* Jason Hunt!

(as, off-stage left, a fiddle starts up – an impromptu rehearsal – joined by a squeeze box. It builds to a reel.)

TOM. 'Pears like they're warming up fer t'night's shindig. That McIver clan – Looky, Miss Hannah –

(He beckons HANNAH to the door. She lays the dress down and goes to stand by him, to look out.)

Looky those young 'uns stompin' it up.

(He raises his arm to point and finds her near. The reel catches him. He starts to move in rhythm. HANNAH feels his nearness.)

HANNAH. Mr. Bowie, I – I think I'd be able to see better outside –

TOM. *(In a burst of hearty fun.)* Sure ye would – !

(He grabs her hand and half pulls her through the

doorway, stage left.)

(Slowly **JASON** *fingers the medicine belt, his eyes on* **RUTH**.*)*

*(***RUTH*** stands uncomfortably aware of him and the silence between them. She looks over the torn dress.)*

(Outside, the jollity of the jig music.)

JASON. Ruth?

RUTH. I – I suppose you've made up your mind?

JASON. Ruth, Look at me.

(She looks up and, in a burst of desperation, runs to him, clinging.)

RUTH. Jason! Jason!

(He kisses her fully. She holds to him almost violently.)

All day – all day I've been wondering: Will he leave me? Will he go? Does he love me?...O, do you, Jason? Do you?

(He holds her, soothing.)

If you left me, Jason – I – I don't know what I'd do. I need you, Jason. And if I ever lost you –

JASON. You'll never lose me, Ruth. Never so long as you love me.

RUTH. O, I do, Jason. I do! I knew that last spring when I saw you – the way you came back – stumbling across the field – your shirt black with blood – the arrow in your shoulder – your head – I died, Jason, seeing you then. But there aren't any Indians in Congress, Jason. I don't have to be afraid how you'll come home – or wonder if you will. You'll be safe there, Jason. Safe for me to love.

(As **JASON** *stiffens, hearing her.)*

Is that so wrong, Jason, wanting you to be safe?

(Slowly he lets her go, looking at her.)

Jason?

JASON. Then it's not – what these people need or want, is it, Ruth? You don't really care about them, do you? Or Craig – ?

RUTH. No! I don't! Not about them! Only you, Jason – !

I'm afraid for you –

JASON. And yet you've been telling me what a real, good thing it'd be. "These people need you," you said. "Go to Congress. It's what you were meant for – "

RUTH. It is!

JASON. You don't believe that.

RUTH. I do!

JASON. No, you don't, Ruth. Not really. You only say that because it's easier than seeing the truth. It's not me you're afraid for, Ruth. It's you! It's *you* yourself that wants to be safe!

(RUTH listens, fingering nervously at BLUNDER's pack.)

Ruth…love isn't something that starts from being safe. Not the way *you* mean it. Like something to run away to – to hide behind. It starts off spanking new – like morning. Like going west. Like – going into something you ain't sure what. And all you've got is what you are – what the good Lord meant ye t' be – and somebody standing tall and sure beside ye, sharing whatever is… trusting in ye. That's all we have, Ruth. That's all we'll ever really need. And that's where we start. Don't ye see that, Ruth? You are safe then. Whatever is, you're safe then.

RUTH. No!

JASON. Ruth? Don't ye love me enough t' trust in me?

(A beat.)

No. Ye don't, do ye? You don't trust me or you or anyone! I bet you don't even trust God!

RUTH. Jason!

JASON. Remember that day on Glory Peak? It almost happened then –

RUTH. *No!*

(A beat.)

JASON. No. I reckon not. I'm sorry, Ruth.

RUTH. Jason, I do love you.

JASON. Do you, Ruth? Remember the Bible: "Whither thou

goest, I will go"? Can you say that, Ruth?

(*A beat.*)

Ruth, if it had been love – But it wasn't, was it? What you wanted – Ye're a lot like Sary, I guess.

(*A beat. Then, decided.*)

I'm taking those people to Zion, Ruth.

RUTH. (*Sharply.*) And what about me? You said you loved me –

JASON. I do, Ruth. Only –

RUTH. (*Rigidly.*) Only what, Jason?

JASON. I'd want a woman, Ruth.

(*The shock hits. With one swift crash of anger, **RUTH** hurls **BLUNDER**'s pack hard into **JASON**'s face.*)

(*The pack falls apart, pelts, trinkets, personal gear scattering about –*)

(*As **HANNAH** and **TOM** come laughing in, winded and hot. They tense immediately at the scene before them.*)

(*Slowly, silently **JASON** bends down and starts collecting **BLUNDER**'s things together.*)

(***HANNAH** goes to **RUTH** who stands rigid and apart, her mouth drawn tight.*)

HANNAH. Ruth?

RUTH. Hannah, help me pack. I'm going back, Hannah. Back – where I belong – Boston –

(*Suddenly, a child's demand.*)

I want to go home, Hannah.

(***JASON** meets **HANNAH**'s look evenly, then goes on gathering up **BLUNDER**'s things.*)

(*Suddenly **TOM** picks up a bear-claw neckpiece.*)

TOM. Jason, look!

JASON. (*Awed.*) Broken Moon's neckpiece. Then he really did kill Broken Moon.

HANNAH. Blunder?

TOM. Thunder Knife!

(*Only **RUTH** shows no interest. She stands cold and*

rigid beside **HANNAH** – *)*

(As offstage and distant, the sharp blasts of a steamboat whistle and the long drawn cry of "Steamboat 'round the bend!" are heard.)

(CURTAIN)

ACT TWO

(**TIME:** *An hour later.*)

(**JASON** *slouches in the chair, lost in frowning thought.*)

(**HANNAH** – *now dressed for travel* – *stands leaning against the door as if memorizing the scene outside.*)

(**BLUNDER**, *perched on a bale, down stage right, runs the bear-claw neckpiece through his fingers.*)

(*From offstage right, noises from the back room – a pan scraping,* **SARY** *humming in a grating, tuneless way, "Billy Boy."*)

(**JASON** *shifts in his chair.*)

JASON. She wouldn't even talk t' me. Acted so funny.

HANNAH. I know. She didn't say a word all during the packing.

JASON. Everything's ready?

HANNAH. There wasn't much to pack.

JASON. I never saw her acting that way before.

HANNAH. It wasn't your fault, Jason. Not really.

(*A beat.*)

JASON. How much time ye got?

HANNAH. Half-an-hour maybe.

BLUNDER. Glad t' be goin', I reckon

(*He eases to his feet.*)

HANNAH. Glad? I'll whistle all the way.

(*Offstage right,* **SARY** *starts to sing and hits a cracked note, one among many.*)

BLUNDER. (*Shouting.*) Sary!

SARY. (*Offstage, sweetly.*) Yes, Blunder?

BLUNDER. Stop that in-fernal cacklin'!

(*A beat.*)

SARY. (*Offstage.*) Why, o' course, Blunder.

BLUNDER. Enough t' crack my ear-pans.

SARY. *(offstage. Nicely.)* Blunder, how d' ye want yer eggs?

BLUNDER. *(a snap of the whip)* Cooked!

(Offstage, the crash of a pan – possibly fallen.)

BLUNDER. Are ye sure, Jason, ye really want t' give me that land?

JASON. It won't be doin' me any good, Blunder. It's yers. Flat and outright – yers – like the paper says.

BLUNDER. It sure changes things.

JASON. *(Rising. Restless.)* Tom should've been here by now. Reckon he went t' the school with her?

HANNAH. No. He just took the trunk to the landing. She went to the school by herself. Said she wanted to.

BLUNDER. What fer?

HANNAH. To close it up.

JASON. Maybe you should've gone with her.

HANNAH. I asked. But she said no.

JASON. She started that school. All by herself.

BLUNDER. What about the young 'uns now?

HANNAH. They'll have to get another teacher.

BLUNDER. Where from? They're scarcer than feathered eggs out here.

(He puts the neckpiece on the counter and, finding another piece of crate wood, takes out his knife and settles back on a keg to whittle.)

HANNAH. I don't know, Blunder.

BLUNDER. If'n ye ask me, I think she's wrong!

HANNAH. It runs in the family, Blunder. At top speed!

BLUNDER. But Ruthie there –

*(Tensely, **JASON** starts towards the back room.)*

BLUNDER. Where ye goin'?

JASON. Out fer water. I – I'm pure dry.

(He strides out, stage right.)

BLUNDER. He's real set on 'er, ain't he?

HANNAH. Yes, Blunder. Real set.

BLUNDER. Miss Hannah, hev ye ever been in love?

HANNAH. Once.

BLUNDER. That's all?! Once?!

HANNAH. For a Bostonian, Blunder, once is a record.

BLUNDER. But – how'd ye know it was love?

HANNAH. Why, Blunder?

BLUNDER. Miss Hannah – if you was in love with a man – and ye was both a-walkin' down by the Creek – down where everythin's so pretty and sweet-smellin', and spring was a-winkin' up at ye – what'd ye do?

HANNAH. I – don't know, Blunder. It's never happened.

BLUNDER. But if'n it did –

HANNAH. If it did?…If it did, I'd talk about how much I loved him. About how proud I'd be that a man like that could love me. I'd talk about the smile in his eyes when he looked at me…and the way it is when we don't need words – only a look…And I think – I'd reach up my hand – and loosen my hair – and let it cover his arms about me…And we'd kiss –

BLUNDER. *(Crashing through.)* Yep! That's what I thought it'd be like, too. But it weren't! All she could do was talk on that dag-blasted land Jason's give me. Ye know, Miss Hannah, I got me a feelin' about Sary –

*(**TOM** enters, stage left.)*

Howdy, Tom.

TOM. Jason here yet?

BLUNDER. Out'n back. Gettin' a drink.

TOM. *(Crossing to stage right.)* Hey, Jason!

*(Turning to **HANNAH**.)*

The trunks're all on board, Miss Hannah. I checked 'em myself.

HANNAH. Thank you, Mr. Bowie.

TOM. You won't be so lonesome now, goin' back with Ruthie. She's all right, ain't she?

HANNAH. She will be – once she's on her way.

BLUNDER. *(As **TOM** glances back to the door, stage right.)* You look kinda worrified, Tom.

TOM. They ain't gonna let Jason go.

(*As* **JASON** *enters, stage right.*)

JASON. Who ain't?

TOM. McIver. He got wind o' yer goin' t' Jefferson, and he's aimin' t' stop ye. Got the whole town stirred up. Says they're gonna get ye t' Congress if'n they got t' boot ye all the way. Even talkin' on shootin' up Craig a bit so's ye'll have t' go –

HANNAH. But they wouldn't –

TOM. You don't know McIver, Miss Hannah. Figures on gettin' Jason out o' the way till after he's elected.

(*To* **JASON.**)

They're gonna do the stumpin' fer ye –

HANNAH. But that's not legal – is it?

TOM. McIver figures it'll work. He's got his mind set on it.

(*To* **JASON.**)

He's got his men all set up, a-waitin'. Looky out there – 'cross the road. Them two there. They're McIver's. Followed me all the way from the landing.

HANNAH. Watching you?

TOM. Closer'n winter hawks.

HANNAH. (*To* **JASON.**) But I thought McIver was your friend – ?

JASON. He sure is.

TOM. Ye'd better see McIver, Jason.

JASON. I'd been thinkin' on that.

(*A beat.*)

You, Tom: you just sorta amble over here so's they can see ye. Make off ye're talkin' t' me – don't look out! – Just easy-like. Like we're just a-jawin' here. I don't want 'em t' get the idea o' skittin' 'round t' the back. I'm gonna get me t' the stables.

TOM. (*Leaning in the doorway.*) But what about McIver?

JASON. First the horses. Then McIver.

TOM. But –

JASON. *(Crossing to the door, stage right.)* Just keep it light and easy-like.

(He exits.)

HANNAH. They're starting to play cards.

TOM. Good!

HANNAH. But – won't there be others watching the stables?

TOM. Yep. Reckon they might.

HANNAH. Then – ?

TOM. 'Minds me a' the time Jason and me got taken by Comanches. Fought through the whole pack of 'em – just t' get to a single hoss. We made it, though.

*(To **BLUNDER**.)*

But we could've used you, Blunder. You and that knife o' yers…. How come ye told Sary that whopper – about killin' 'em with a fiddlestring?

BLUNDER. Well – I figgered anybody coulda done it with a knife. Besides, I didn't want folks knowin' who I was. I didn't want t' be Thunder Knife no more. Everywhere's I'd go, folks'd know who I was. And they'd just stare at me so questiferous-like, I got t' feelin' I warn't human no more. I got tired a' that. I wanted t' settle down. Sorta ease out my time, quiet and gentle-like. So I growed this here beard and changed my clothes some, and took my real name – and – nobody knowed me. And then I come here. And I seed Sary.

(A beat.)

She was just a-flailing and a whippin' at a pore little ten-foot peddlar, 'peared like. Reckon he must-a tried t' gyp 'er some – Well, here were Sary, just a tearin' into him, sparks a-flyin' and words a-cussin' – so I says t' myself, Now, there, Blunder, 's a real spunky woman fer ye. She's got spirit, I says – and then I got t' thinkin'. She's the woman fer ye, Blunder…Only –

TOM. Only what, Blunder?

BLUNDER. Ever since ye 'minded me of 'er, I keep thinkin' on Laughin' Sky. I kept thinkin' on 'er all the way back from the Creek. She liked me – just as I was. I keep seein' her eyes, and the way she walked – and the way she smelled – like summer in high meadows. And standin' there, she 'minded me o' birch trees shinin' by clear blue lake water – Do she still walk proud, Tom?

TOM. Proud as a princess.

BLUNDER. She *is* a princess.

TOM. Yeah. I know. That makes yer son a prince now, don't it?

BLUNDER. Yeah. It do, don't it?

(Suddenly, vehemently.)

But – But things is changed now! I'm changed! I'm –

(He breaks off with a sharp cry, seeing **HANNAH** *holding up the bear-claw neckpiece as if to put it on.)*

Miss Hannah! DON'T – !!

HANNAH. *(Startled, drops the neckpiece.)* Blunder!

BLUNDER. *(Crossing to pick it up from the counter.)* Didn't mean t' frighten ye none, Miss Hannah. It's just dangerous-like – foolin' around with this here medicine piece.

HANNAH. Medicine piece?

BLUNDER. 'Bout the biggest medicine this side the moon.

HANNAH. *(Uneasily.)* Honestly, Blunder –

BLUNDER. I ain't a-foolin', Miss Hannah.

(Showing the neckpiece closely.)

Ye see all these here bear claws? Well, they ain't just bear claws, Miss Hannah. They're real, honest-t'-goodness spirits!

TOM. Bear're mighty big spirits in these here parts, Miss Hannah.

BLUNDER. The biggest they is, I reckon. Every claw here means ye got a bear spirit around ye all the time. And this 'un here's got a hundred an' nine of 'em. Good or bad – dependin' –

HANNAH. On what?

BLUNDER. On when ye first wears it. That's why I ain't give it t' Sary yet. I gotta wait till the moon comes full.

HANNAH. The moon?

BLUNDER. Three days from now.

TOM. The night o' the full moon, Miss Hannah. That's sorta the sacred time o' the Great Bear Spirit.

BLUNDER. Ye see, ye put this on by the light o' the full moon so's he can see it, like. And then he'll make everyone o them hundred-an'-nine bear spirits go with ye all yer life – just a-tearin' and a-scrappin' and a-fightin' off all yer miseries fer ye so's ye won't have a single one t' fret ye.

HANNAH. And – if you don't wait for the full moon?

BLUNDER. Why, then that Great Bear Spirit there – he'd be real put out, I reckon, and that'd make him pure onery. And, Miss Hannah, they ain't nothin' onerier than an onery bear. So he'd just up and make everyone of them bear spirits start t' clawin' away at ye. They'd just up and claw yer heart right out, Miss Hannah. Claw it right out with the miseries.

HANNAH. Mr. Bowie, do you believe all this?

TOM. No. But I wouldn't go wearin' it, neither.

SARY. *(Offstage. Sweetly.)* Blunder. Yer dinner's ready.

BLUNDER. *(Sheathing his knife.)* Don't know's I'm hungry now.

(He exits, stage right.)

(A beat.)

HANNAH. *(Touching the neckpiece on the counter.)* It didn't help Broken Moon any, did it?

TOM. Maybe because Death's bigger than the Great Bear Spirit…Hannah –

HANNAH. Back in Salem they would have –

TOM. I love ye, Hannah.

(A beat.)

HANNAH. Thank you, Mr. Bowie.

TOM. I never said that before.

HANNAH. I know.

TOM. Hannah, ye can't go now.

HANNAH. I can't let Ruth go alone. Not the way she is.

TOM. That ain't all the truth.

HANNAH. The – The mountains are too – too near, Mr. Bowie. Too sudden – !

TOM. You could take them in your stride, Hannah.

HANNAH. If I had time – maybe –

TOM. I'd wait on ye, Hannah.

HANNAH. But you haven't known me a day – You've only seen me –

TOM. Hannah, I know…Just as you know –

HANNAH. But –

TOM. Hannah, don't ye want to?

HANNAH. *(desperately)* Tom! Tom – !

(Offstage, SL. A cry of warning.)

BAILEY. Look out! Miss Ruth – !

*(**HANNAH** whirls as **RUTH** enters, SL, her movements slow, trance-like, as she leans heavily against the wall just inside the door.)*

*(**HANNAH** approaches, fearful, concerned.)*

HANNAH. Ruth?…Ruth, what's wrong?

RUTH. All the desks were empty…I just stood there…looking…smelling the chalk-dust…It seemed so small…so dim…like a make-believe school-room. Like the one in Mama's attic back home…where we used to play school.

(She moves vaguely towards the chair, near center.)

I started to walk to my desk. But I never got there. I couldn't. I sat at one of the little desks…

(As she sits, primly.)

…as if I were a child sitting there…like – just a little girl…And all the while I kept thinking of little Tony Rankin…his face scrubbed shiny…that star-bright look in his eyes. "We're going west, Miss Toby." – He was going west. And I – I was running home…like a little girl…. That's all I am, Hannah!…A little girl running home to be safe…! Safe in snug, little patterns…where after Sunday, Monday comes – with Monday things to do…

HANNAH. Ruth –

(She starts to go to her, but TOM holds her back gently.)

RUTH. …Where you can grow up to be – a little girl all your life…and there's no one to know…or care…like Jason.

(Turning abruptly.)

I was ready to pull Jason under, Tom! I – I didn't mean to. I wanted him to be safe! And I – I believed it.

(Slowly she stands.)

But Jason knew. He tore them away – the lies I hid behind. I wasn't afraid for him. I was afraid for myself! …If he went west – I'm afraid of going west, Tom! I don't know what it's like out there, and I'm afraid of what I don't know – !

BLUNDER. *(Offstage. A bellow of anger.)* Sary!

SARY. *(Offstage.)* But, Blunder-honey –

(As BLUNDER storms in, stage right, his napkin still tucked under his chin – followed by SARY.)

SARY. I only said we could make a heap a' money out'n that land –

BLUNDER. *(Whipping the napkin away.)* That land! – I don't know's I even want it!

SARY. Jason said it was yers!

BLUNDER. What fer? I don't need it.

SARY. But we do.

BLUNDER. Sary, I ain't never seed a woman like you before.

(He jams the napkin into her hand.)

SARY. Ye don't have t' say Yes right now, Blunder –

BLUNDER. Sary, I don't have t' say Yes no-time.

SARY. 'Course not, Blunder. But – let's go fer a walk – later on – just you and me – and look at that land –

BLUNDER. That land! That's all ye been talkin' on, Sary. That land! Like I was nothing!

SARY. Now, Blunder –

BLUNDER. But I am, Sary. I am something!

(He turns, moving about, with tribal grandeur.)

They talk on me 'round injun campfires. They tell as how I'm a spirit. They got stories o' me – 'bout things I never done – no man could ever do. But they think I could do 'em –

SARY. 'Course ye could, Blunder –

BLUNDER. And they's dances – and they's songs fer me – You heared 'em, ain't ye, Tom?

(Slowly he raises his arms in an upward sweep, his voice eerie and deep, a strange, glittering light in his eyes, the warrior's Song of Himself.)

Brother o' the west wind.

Son o' the summer storms.

Claw o' the Manitou…

Thunder Knife!

(He stands a moment in the glory of himself.)

SARY. Now, ain't that somethin', Tom?

BLUNDER. Yep. It is, Sary. Somethin' t' be real proud on. Only – I never seed it like that before. And here I was a-tryin' t' be somethin' I ain't. Like I was ashamed o' bein' me.

(to **TOM***)*

But ye can't go skittin' from things like that, can ye, Tom?

TOM. If a mountain's there, Blunder, there's no good sayin' it ain't.

*(***RUTH** *reacts to this, her look suddenly clearing.)*

SARY. But, Blunder –

BLUNDER. It ain't me ye wants, Sary. It's the land, ain't it?

(He looks at her thoughtfully; then, scratching his beard:)

And all this time I been goin' wrong, thinkin' ye meant somethin' t' me.

SARY. But I do, Blunder –

BLUNDER. No, ye don't, Sary. Not any more ye don't. Not any more'n this here beard do.

(He turns, starting out stage right, drawing his knife.)

SARY. Where ye goin'?

BLUNDER. Out'n back. I somehow sorta feel it's time I shaved.

(He exits, stage right.)

SARY. Blunder – wait –

(She follows, stage right.)

RUTH. It's true, isn't it, Tom? You can't go skitting from things, can you? Not if they're real –

TOM. If a mountain's there –

RUTH. Or an eagle's cry –

TOM. Then it's there.

(Suddenly, from offstage left, noises of a crowd break through. The voices of men over a hubbub.)

FIRST VOICE. *(Offstage.)* Hey, there he is! There's Jason!

SECOND VOICE. *(Offstage.)* Hey, McIver! Jason's here!

THIRD VOICE. *(Offstage.)* Hey, Jason!

FOURTH VOICE. *(Offstage.)* He's got the hosses saddled up!

*(**JASON** backs in, stage left, facing a spill of men who crowd him into the store, as **McIVER** comes through and faces **JASON**.)*

McIVER. Hi-ya, Jason.

JASON. Hi, McIver.

McIVER. Heard ye was runnin' out on us. Heard ye was goin' t' Jefferson.

JASON. Come t' think of it, McIver, I heard something, too. About you wantin' t' shoot up Craig or somethin'.

McIVER. Better'n havin' him get t' Congress, ain't it?

JASON. Somebody's got t' get there.

McIVER. That's what me and the folks here figure. And we kinda figure it's gonna be *you*. Ain't that right, folks?

(Crowd reaction, closing in on **JASON.***)*

FIRST VOICE. Yeah!

SECOND VOICE. It sure is!

THIRD VOICE. That's what we figure.

FOURTH VOICE. That's it, Jason!

FIFTH VOICE. We sure do!

JASON. Now, wait – ! Wait a bit!

(The crowd subsides.)

Ye all came t' town fer the speechin' – right?

FIRST VOICE. That's it!

SECOND VOICE. We sure did.

THIRD VOICE. We aim t' show we're behind ye, Jason!

FOURTH VOICE. All the way t' Congress!

SARY. *(Bustling in from stage right.)* What's goin' on?

JASON. All right! All right now! Listen – 'cause I'm making my speech right here and now.

(He kicks a small crate into place and steps up on it.)

First off, I want you folks t' know I'm mighty obliged t' ye. I'm pure grateful fer what ye've given me – yer friendship and yer trust. And I ain't kicking that away like an ol' empty flour barrel.

(A beat.)

Sure, I'd like t' grow with this here town. I reckon anybody would with folks like you around. But up in Jefferson there's wagon trains a-waitin' – folks wantin' t' grow with a whole new continent. And I want t' help in that growin' –

FIRST VOICE. What's wrong with helpin' in Congress?

SECOND VOICE. Yeah, what's wrong with that?

JASON. Listen! Up in Jefferson, there's four o' them wagon trains – waitin' – just a-waitin' on goin' west. But there's no one t' lead 'em…just Tom and me. And Tom – he can't do it alone. So – if'n I don't go – two o' them trains'll more'n likely set off by themselves – and *you* all know what that means. Now, I don't say I can get 'em through myself. I'm just sayin' they'll have a better chance with me along t' show 'em what I know. To help 'em. Ain't that right, McIver?

McIVER. I reckon so. But we want ye fer Congress!

JASON. That's just my point. You all *want* me fer Congress, but they *need* me in Jefferson!

FIRST VOICE. But that'll mean Craig'll get in – !

SECOND VOICE. He'll just slick his way in –

THIRD VOICE. We sure as heck don't need Craig –

FOURTH VOICE. We don't even want him – !

JASON. Hold it! I ain't sayin' Craig'll get in. I'm just sayin' that while ye may *want* me, what ye really need is – *McIver* here!

McIVER. Me??!!

JASON. Yes, McIver. You! Ye're honest. Ye know what these people want and need. And ye've never turned yer back on a fight – or lost one yet. Has he, folks!

FIRST VOICE. No, he ain't!

SECOND VOICE. McIver!

THIRD VOICE. He'd sure fit – !

McIVER. But I ain't had no schoolin' like you –

JASON. You can read! You can write! You can think! You can do it, McIver! And what you do have – ye can't learn out of books. Use it fer these people.

McIVER. I can't –

JASON. All right, McIver. I'll make you an offer. *You* lead those wagons west, and *I'll* go to Congress.

(A beat.)

McIVER. I reckon I know what ye mean, Jason.

JASON. Ye'll run fer Congress?

(a beat)

McIVER. *(Solemnly.)* I will.

(**JASON** *steps down to shake* **McIVER***'s hand. The crowd reacts, voices shouting "Yeah, McIver!" – "Hey, McIver!" – "McIver fer Congress!" as they surge out the door, SL, herding* **McIVER** *through.*)

(**JASON** *turns to see* **TOM, SARY, HANNAH,** *and* **RUTH** *looking at him, glowing.*)

JASON. The horses' re ready, Tom.

TOM. That were real fine, Jason.

HANNAH. You make an admirable politician, Jason.

SARY. It sure did sound good.

(A beat, as **RUTH** *comes to him, shining.)*

RUTH. McIver is the right man, Jason.

(As **BLUNDER** *enters – with an almost shock effect. He is clean shaven – a ruggedly handsome man of a lively 40 or so. He sets down his pack and rifle and looks about.)*

SARY. *(Awed.)* Blunder!

JASON. What happened to yer beard?

BLUNDER. I couldn't stand it no more.

SARY. *(Hungrily.)* Blunder, you do be the purtiest thing!

TOM. You just don't seem possible no how, Blunder.

BLUNDER. *(Feeling his chin.)* Figgered my squaw wouldn't know me with it on –

SARY. Yer squaw – ?

BLUNDER. *(To* **TOM.***)* She's a-waitin' o me, ain't she, Tom?

TOM. Fer a mighty long time, Blunder. But they's a mess o' Pawnee between you and her, Blunder. They's pure set on gettin' yer scalp.

BLUNDER. Tom, I don't keer if all the injuns this side the Missouri was after me. I'm goin' back fer my family. And mebbe we'll set out fer that Zion place ye've been talkin' on –

SARY. But, Blunder, what about me?

(A beat.)

BLUNDER. Ye know that land ye done give me, Jason?

JASON. Yeah.

BLUNDER. I'd kinda like t' give it t' Sary here –

SARY. Blunder!

BLUNDER. – seein' as how she wants it so bad.

JASON. It's all yers, Blunder. Do whatever ye like.

BLUNDER. *(Taking a crumpled paper from his pocket.)*

Then it's all yers, Sary. All free fer nothin' – Here.

(He hands her the paper.)

SARY. Thank ye, Blunder.

BLUNDER. *(Taking the neckpiece from the counter.)* And this, too, Sary –

SARY. Broken Moon's neckpiece?

BLUNDER. Yep. I want ye should have it, Sary…I want ye should wear it t'night –

HANNAH. But, Blunder –

TOM. *(Sharply.)* Hannah!

BLUNDER. It'd pleasure me, Sary, t' think o' you…a-wearin' that t'night…knowin' what it means.

SARY. *(Clutching it to her.)* I will, Blunder. I promise ye. And thank ye, Blunder. It sure do look purty.

BLUNDER. *(Picking up his long rifle.)* Well, I reckon I'd better get me a hoss, too. Bye, Jason.

JASON. Bye, Blunder.

(As they shake hands.)

BLUNDER. Tom –

TOM. Good luck, Blunder.

(They shake hands.)

Give 'em my love.

BLUNDER. Miss Hannah.

HANNAH. *(Shaking his hand.)* It's been a great pleasure knowing you –

(With a wry smile.)

— Thunder Knife.

BLUNDER. Ruthie?

RUTH. *(A warm hand.)* Thank you, Blunder.

BLUNDER. Fer what?

RUTH. For mountains and eagles.

(A gentle kiss on the cheek.)

Find them, Blunder. And God bless you.

BLUNDER. Ye know – I got me a feelin'. I got it knocked on the head!

(And with a beaming wave, he turns and is gone, SL, as from off-stage the blast of a warning whistle sounds from the steamboat.)

JASON. *(to* **RUTH**) There's the whistle. You'd better hurry, Ruth.

RUTH. Jason, I'm not going back. I know that now…just as I know I'm not a little girl any more in pigtails and pinafores.

(A beat.)

I want to be your woman, Jason – the one who stood beside you on Glory Peak. That's all I want. That's all I'll ever need. To be with you.

JASON. Through injun country?

RUTH. "Whither thou goest, I will go."

(With a bright, glowing laugh of realization, **JASON** *sweeps her into his arms.)*

JASON. Glory hallelujia! Ruth, there's a preacher up in Jefferson –

RUTH. Hannah, you don't mind going back alone, do you?

HANNAH. Back? I – I don't have to go back.

(To **TOM.***)*

I don't. There's a school here – and no teacher –

TOM. Ye're goin' t' stay?

HANNAH. I've never taught school before. But I can learn! I can learn a lot of things – in a year, Tom?

TOM. By next spring, Hannah. I promise!

HANNAH. By next spring.

TOM. Hannah –

(As offstage the second blast of the steamboat whistle sounds.)

SARY. The second whistle –

TOM. We'd better get them trunks off the boat.

(He turns to go, stage left.)

HANNAH. Tom, wait –

(As she hurries to go with him.)

(Laughing, **JASON** *and* **RUTH** *follow.)*

JASON. Good-bye, Sary.

RUTH. Bye, Sary.

(At the door, stage left, **JASON** *and* **RUTH** *pause, tall and proud, looking out.)*

JASON. Blunder was sure right, now, wasn't he? We've got it knocked on the head.

(And joyous, together – as one – they go. **SARY** *stands alone, frowning vaguely about her store. She looks at the neckpiece in her hand, fingering it slowly, as* **HANNAH** *enters – her long hair free and beautiful about her shoulders, her bonnet held by her side.)*

SARY. Hannah, yer hair – !

HANNAH. *(In a glow.)* They're all of them – pure cloud-tall – aren't they, Sary? And a year isn't too long.

*(**SARY** smiles.)*

*(**HANNAH** crosses to the window to watch after them.)*

*(**SARY** sighs, looking at the neckpiece, her eyes darkening.)*

SARY. I'm sure gonna miss Blunder...Kinda miss him already.

(**HANNAH** *turns.*)

(**SARY** *raises the neckpiece, about to put it on.*)

(**HANNAH** *makes a move to stop her, then checks herself, watching, uneasy.*)

SARY. He was the only man that ever gave me anything.

(*Putting on the neckpiece, she fingers it lovingly.*)

…even his love.

HANNAH. Yes. He did give you that, didn't he?

(**HANNAH** *turns again, staring out; then – suddenly, rapt, fixed – *)

(*As* **SARY**, *with a look of jagged hurt, clutches at the neckpiece, as if to tear it off, anguished.*)

SARY. Hannah! Hannah!

(**HANNAH** *turns, a glow of wonder in her eyes, her voice an awed whisper.*)

HANNAH. I saw it, Sary…Just over there in the woods…I saw it! *The snow-white buck!*

(*CURTAIN*)

COSTUMES

Women
Act I
SARY - 1830 ordinary homespun dress, dull grey
HANNAH - Fashionable 1830 traveling dress, blue
RUTH - 1830 mourning dress, simple, black

Act II
HANNAH - Same as Act I, but with shawl and bonnet
RUTH - Same as Act I, but with shawl

Men
JASON - 1830 frontiersman garb: buckskin, mocassins
MCIVER - (and his men) 1830 backwoodsmen garb: britches, homespun shirts, ordinary make-shift garb, boots
BLUNDER - 1830 frontiersman garb, much like JASON's, but shabby, scarred. A belt for his sheath and knife. Mocassins.
TOM - 1830 frontiersman garb: leather britches, sheep-skin jacket (on entry); homespun shirt, heavy boots

PROPERTIES

Special
Wampum belt
Bear-claw neckpiece
Hun-ting knife
1830 long rifle (to be used by both TOM and BLUNDER)
A crudely painted banner: JASON HUNT FOR CONGRESS
A Tory Flag, time-battered

General
Liniment and cloths (for Act I)
For SARY's store: loose pelts, various barrels and kegs; shelfstock - bottles, packaged goods, bales, pots, pans, etc., for sale or display, etc.
Various chairs, a bench, a table or two

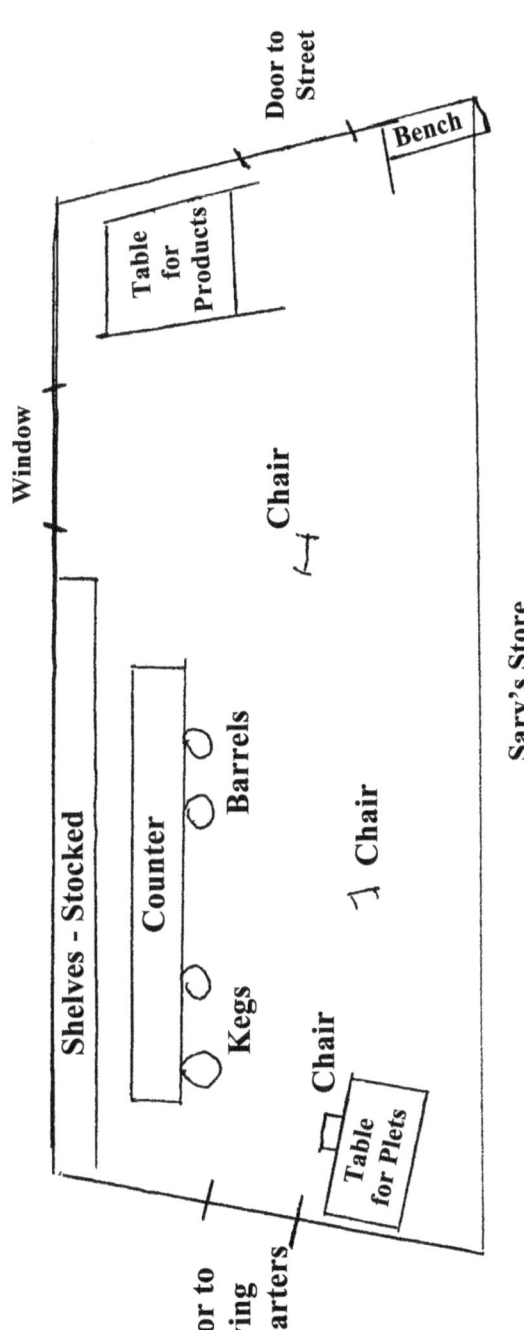

www.ingramcontent.com/pod-product-compliance
Lightning Source LLC
Chambersburg PA
CBHW071843290426
44109CB00017B/1912